RECLAIMED WATER

RECLAIMED WATER

TOM SNARSKY

///
///

ORNITHOPTER PRESS   PRINCETON

First Edition

Published by Ornithopter Press
www.ornithopterpress.com

ISBN 978-1-942723-14-1

Library of Congress Control Number: 2023936478

Cover image:
The Garden of Death, 1896
by Hugo Simberg

Design and composition by Mark Harris

Contents

two

water and speech
space you have to believe in it

—Anne-Marie Albiach
tr. Peter Riley

RECLAIMED WATER

Bad news comes in threes
Morning, noon, & night

Round stones in the river
Weren't always that way

To a star
A tree lives a fast life

Eventually moons forget
What they were doing before

one

Saddest Factory

Love, the place to be
my smallest self
without fear, is close
to the old factory
where they used to make
buttons—not the kind
you push to make
something happen,
but the kind you
turn sideways to
slip through a hole
& fasten. Lucky I
know that, since I don't
have a map. It was told
to me by someone very
far away from us now,
Mars-far, but not
in a billionaire way
more of a ladies-and-
gentlemen-we-are-floating-
in-space kind of
way. The hot lie
of a Florida afternoon.
I don't know, February
seems so distant
now too, like a remote
northern lake you've never seen
thaw, or known to.

I Don't Know, Black Fog?

Stilts?
Forgettable exes?
A lavender
Moon?
Tomatoes
As a boundary case
In elementary school?
A doctorate
In veterinary medicine?
Good reasons?
Hands
That are so soft?

KB Toys

The stars are fishing
for compliments, no clouds

& the kind of cold that makes
you remember stars are *hot*,

or were, however long ago
they shined the light you are

seeing, maybe at their hottest
& about to die—I

remember the yo-yo
section, Duncan Yomega

Yoyofactory MAGIC YOYO
I know one card trick but you

have to have exactly 10
letters in the magic word

for it to work so
sometimes I fudge it

with initials or
whatever spell out

something nearby & if I can't
find anything

I just use my name

Outer Tactics

Spinning Sibylle
Baier's *Colour
Green*, or
really it's
on Spotify
to be
more honest
about modes
of transport
of information,
the sound
going in
a cache
instead of
circling below
a needle,
vestigial record
like a
water wheel
turning and
turning over
the stream
one side
of its
white oak
faded by
the sun
but none
of this
can tell
you anything

about her
voice, Sibylle's,
how it
took nearly
30 years
for *Colour*
Green's songs
to make
it out
to people,
ghost voice
carried into
the new
century by
a son—
now I'm
getting ahead
of myself
the songs
are just
beautiful, were
recorded between
1970 and
1973 with
minimal accompaniment,
mostly, stored
thereafter until
Sibylle's son
Robby made
a CD
of them
and gave
one to

J Mascis,
rest is
history etc.
I have
never written
about how
my mom
is a
singer, was
in all
manner of
bands over
the years
and recorded
on three
occasions: "Don't
Be Shy"
in 1988,
"Center Stage"
in I
forget what
year, and
"Sands of
Time" in
I also
forget, something
funny searching
"sands of
time" in
your email,
hoping for
what exactly
the video

we made
for it,
mom's song,
Bob had
big ideas
that shaped
it but
the song
is hers,
intellectual property
law notwithstanding
(my mom
is also
a lawyer)—
a forest
gave itself
a name
and now
we're here.
Today I
couldn't remember
my father's
hands, Kristi
asked me
what rings
he wore
band of
late gold
on the
horizon near
sunset, evening
an inkling
waiting for

its quill
forgetting is
nothing like
baseball on
the radio
in which
they tell
you repeatedly
who's where
because you
cannot see
Stevie Nicks
rehearsing "Wild
Heart" in
the makeup
chair singing
her heart
out "I
kind of
hate the
word 'heart'"
Ben Mirov
says somewhere
silent seas
Richter's Rachmaninoff's
(Op. 32
No. 10)
sustain pedal
with poets
it's always
the line
break and
never the

brake line
foolish heart
pumping fluid
for ever
god's water
wheels intercepting
just enough
blood to
keep us
lit illumine
the marian
brain "immaculate
etymology" I
googled trying
to continue
my dad
always loved
that one
Staind song

Shadow Barbarian (short mix)

green glass moon

Junk Philosophy

A lake bottomed with copper
so the radio waves can't
get through to the groundwater,
no talking to the aquifer, no
dissuading it from providing
the one thing we need

Reflection

The trees have the lake
fully surrounded

so the lake makes like
it's holding the sun

hostage

Pierrot lunaire

I.

Andromeda
A brief flare
Fucking
Up the field

This will only take a moment

II.

I have an experiment running
On grief

Wine & regretful food
Lives separate
In the centrifuge

Larksong

III.

Ordinary
Rain cup

Filling

IV.

Half a day
Later the trees
Are paper

Signed
Like numbers

Wet & you
See through it

V.

Where, my love

VI.

Fumigator ocean
Jellyfish lying

Ancient star

VII.

X

VIII.

I marry
The new cloud

The new type
Of cloud

I marry
My cloud

IX.

Before the planets formed
Before spheres & life

There was still weight
There was still waiting

& sand

X.

Blessed sacrament
Of holding all time
In your craw

XI.

Fucking up
The field
Is a little crime

François Villon
Gets away with
Every day
He stays dead

XII.

You do not owe any of us anything

Blue river

XIII.

Bread of life

XIV.

coign of vantage

And if sun comes
How shall we greet him?
　　—Gwendolyn Brooks

it's 30 minutes until sunset
when i will post the picture i took
of "lebensweisheitspielerei"
i had been missing the things i
usually touched, including
that big unwieldy faber & faber
collected poems of wallace stevens
that lived in my car
in the center console
the way poetry could steal
a few minutes between tasks
idling in one of america's few
remaining parking lots
(hard(l)y har har)
the way touch made it more possible
to just thumb a poem
for a moment, like a protective thimble
against the blowback
of the world
its repeated needle jabs
this thimble thought brought me to
(but first i hope you check out
the wikipedia page for thimbles,
it's really the gold standard)
touch pieces, i.e.
little talismans of medicine & luck
kings & queens rubbing coins
on the heads of the sick
to heal them

(if it didn't work
then you simply were not
faithful enough)
it's a short citational road from the touch piece
to the mercury dime
famous american instance of same
the god of commerce on a coin
which of course would be the irony
here but it's even better, that the front
of the mercury dime is really meant
to be a picture of liberty
's bust, & everyone just mistook
liberty for mercury
almost as american a confusion
(freedom for the mercurial;
god just think of insurance)
as doing your own work on company time
or the brute fact of a parking lot
our flattest terraformation
if the parking lot is the actual
physical space i return to the most
for writing then the idea
-space i return to the most
in poems
is the sea
i grew up near one
& just read for the first time
greta wrolstad's
"notes on sea & shore" it showed me
how much i still have to learn
about this craft
on its open water
wikipedia is generous

with the terminology for oceans
lakes rivers all the lands
& land formations
incident to them
i learned that a ria
is not air or a song but instead
a drowned river valley
though to see something so close
to aria put me in mind of stevens
cartoonish operatic
great lover of islands
& a seller of insurance
there are so many names for cliffs
did you know "coign of vantage"
means "a favourable position
for observation or action"
funny that metal currency
reënters our ear here
& i could've sworn stevens had a poem
actually called "aria"
sharon olds sharon olds
but searching i found instead
the are-you-fucking-with-me? fact
that his wife elsie was the model
for the mercury dime
the selfsame one
an instance of which i bought
on ebay
for a dollar after the touch piece affair
i carry it with me every day now
just to see if
like the other sacred coins of lore
faithfulness helps

it to heal
mine's a '42 so i'm starting with parts
of a world the stevens book from that year
it & sharon olds both born in the same revolution
while the world was being made
violently aware
of its parts
to figure out what the fuck exactly
the universe is trying to tell me
with this confluence
not all these researches have been done
in parking lots
stevens was a role model in almost nothing
except stealing time from work to write
the french say *faire*
de la perruque literally making
of the wig
doing one's own work
on company time
i'm writing this now during a class
the kids are in their breakout rooms
i am being the worst
version of myself qua teacher
sitting on my remote little shore all helen
in egypt
my achilles a stubborn sea bird
merzbow's new album screaming dove
is out soon & not far
into parts of a world we read
"[p]oet, patting more nonsense foamed
[f]rom the sea," three lines down
from a reminder of why
stevens is such a racist disaster

called Gwendolyn Brooks a horrible name
thought mussolini should take
ethiopia & yet Gwendolyn Brooks herself casts
in 1955
the deciding vote
to give an earlier version
of the very book in my hands
the national book award
(is this true?)
the ceremony is
three months after
the murder of emmett till
sharon olds's aria for trayvon martin
po(u)ring like hot milk from the future
& whiteness lets me mark time like this
do my little historiography
of poetry & grief
& who won what award(s) & when
defer to gilded poets like stevens
or bronk who worked unfettered
in "snug unawareness" (Brooks again)
built their arks before 9
after 5
perchance between
only had sense & meaning
to worry about
were not scared of money
or property
didn't have to be
greta's poem of the sea
begins "[a]s for gold's effect
on the first white men
on this continent,

a Nahuatlan scribe said
they fingered it
as if their hearts
were illumined
[&] made new"
[my removal
of the italics]
my '42 mercury hums
from its dime bag
in my wallet
entitlement of touch
of holding
a need to seal off
from others
greta's poem continues "we
are all unmoored", sure
but the mooring of starting out
is imperfectly shared
in america of its white lines
in parking lots
its spotty healthcare coverage
& sunsets
today's instance of which
is two minutes earlier
than yesterday's
stevens's blue-green pines
bronk's blue spruces watch
the change, those
slow sentries of sun
range rover sentinel
a headline from last year reads
"[t]he market for bulletproof vehicles
is exploding" all that

ballistic steel plating
with beautiful souls inside
do you think a teacher could afford
a bulletproof car
just smudged the stevens collected's
white cover with oil grease
bc Kristi & i changed the driver rear tire
on my 2003
toyota camry
xle
the first & only car i've ever bought
with teaching money
very susceptible
to gunfire
luckily (???) with covid, remote learning
a school shooting would require
very ambitious bullets
maybe i'd be lucky
& get fired on
with my mercury dime in my breast
pocket so just like with roosevelt's notes
& glasses case
i'd be ok
teach an 80-minute class after
hell, 84
this poem is now very current events
the event being one long unfurling
american violence
& the current being mitigated
by the splitting
of the ria
hopping delta islands
on a pogo stick

look carefully
it's nearly 5:55
the sunset's coming
do you see it from your little white cliff
removed from all the rushing
of the water do you see it
from your little
white cliff
do you
& if you do
if you do see it
what are you
& your shiny coin
your shiny coin
not of gold
going to do about it
about the fact that all my friends don't have
insurance, about "the regulation of
weights and rates
in the marketplace" (jack sharpless)
to which must be lent
"discerning,
personal attention"
(sharpless again)
all these poets dying young
sharpless at 38
wrolstad at 24
Brooks at 83 (still too soon)
snarsky at tbd
louise glück agreed with bonnefoy
a poet is a joke of a thing
to call yourself
you save it for your heroes

climbing their thin-limbed trees in the dark
balancing enough to report
what Brooks somewhere
calls "tender grandeur"
the golden light on the wavecrests
the purple martins
a screaming dove
about halfway through
parts of a world we have:
"[t]wo people, three horses, an ox
[a]nd the sun, the waves together in the sea"
compare the bronk
of "midsummer":
in certain pictures, envied landscapes are seen
(through a window, maybe)
like quotation marks
do you think bronk ever really found love
in his life
love subs in for art
almost naturally
in his last poem:
love isn't made; it's in the world almost
unseen but found existent there
like gentle crushes
like risk
like an ashrita furman guinness world record
for watermelons sliced
on the stomach in one minute
the tragedy of only having an emoji
for watermelon that is already sliced up
the little seeds like delta islands
amidst embarrassment
river-red

Poem

I slept through the room, ended up on fire. It had been a short dream.
Wiping the spit from the violin's mouth, hand-washing the silicone.
The *t* in *softening* softening, almost to nothing at all.

The Virginia Opossum

The ladder to my death led to a hole full
of wasps that, once we patched it, buzzed
like crummy neon. A good sign should

hum, not buzz, I learned—transformers
that are too old or overloaded make
the lights buzz, or burn out entirely. I'm

65% sure Howie, *not* one of the
possums, is eating the cat food I
leave out at night. I look at like 10:30

and it's already half-gone; the possums
are much slower, more casual eaters
maybe because of the way their hands

can only hold a few pieces of food
at a time. Howie is one of the biggest
cats I have ever seen in my life,

and it's honestly a little scary
when he just sits at the door for
an hour and a half after we've fed him,

like he's making a mental inventory
of all the amenities inside
cats get to enjoy without coursing

through the high grasses,
picking up ticks like nature's silica gel—
small, firm, plasticky & obscenely

rounded, + enough of them and you'd be dry
as the ancient paper of a yellow jacket
nest, with all its bloodless integrity before

the possum, underfed & unafraid
of any sting, crashes through

The Roses of Heliogabalus

The wind plays a small game with the trees. A win, a loss,
a night. The rules are cops in the grass. My heart is a moon
that is too late to change. The drop from cliff to sea is not a
big one. High rocks taunt the air. I wish I was more *clean*, I
don't know. More like stone that has met sand. I'm a fixed
time on a smashed watch; all day I wait to be right, twice,
then I die to the sound of the waves.

Feeling adulthood's sequence of tasks
heaven, no that doesn't mean *get heavy*
at all, nevermind—feeling it split
dailiness into two moments, one of looking
at your phone & the other of heaving
a great big deeply silly brain-homunculus sigh
—it's like being in a garden, big as Versailles
with one little 75¢ seed packet of wildflowers
in your pocket. The garden supply
is closed & not within walking distance anyway
so even your brief fantasia on the idea
of bricking the window to steal one of the least
expensive goods they sell is sad-tinged. 2nite
you will put on the bright harness of evening
& maybe leave
without telling anyone, at least in your head
where there's a party & people to cry to.
A whole silvering ocean of names:
A, B, C, ... Z, AA, AB, & the silhouette
of a seagull you saw on the shower wall
after you halfheartedly suctioned the water-
proof radio to it, the one you never use.

I proved I didn't have the stomach for being
the kind of person who can quote Spinoza
from memory, the scholia rhyming instead
with an old crush's preferred brand of chew,
we are by no means free in respect to what
we seek, but of course I didn't remember that,
I looked it up, how well did I hide that I needed
help? Maybe it's become too easy to forget
that this is a *technology*, a foolish tool
like some of the body's most shameful
attractions, or like fire, which you'd switch to
for cigarettes, unctuous smoke in the backlog
of so many nights like when we were both
drunk & we drove around the corner for some
reason, literally just to talk about nothing
your handle of Malibu right by the gearshift
& a cop grazing in the church parking lot

sorry I'm here now

I was just at the shame store

returning something

Song of Restoration

for Kristi

In the chandelier hospital
I've been sleeping on a little cot
attending the mysteries
of healing. You are still
dazzling, but in fragments;—
everywhere a hint of a whole.

September is saying its long goodbye
as ants march up the juice box.
Most planets are probably so
much quieter than ours.
You are sleeping. I am looking
at your face and seeing it as
night's greatest gift: the slack that
with diamonds or glass
throws light all over the room.

What Can & Cannot Pass Thru The Green Glass Door

A happy person, but not a sad person. Grass, but not flowers. A flotilla of ships, but not an army. Bullets, but not a gun. A needle, but not its syringe. Sadness, but not death. Parallel lines, but not perpendicular. A sunny day, but not a rainy one. Floors, but not ceilings. Rotten fruit, but not fresh. Pebbles, but not the sand. The Gospel of Matthew, but not the Gospel of John. The Book of Revelations, but not the Song of Songs. A cello, but not a violin. Olivier Messiaen, but not his birds. "An Occurrence at Owl Creek Bridge", but not *The Red Badge of Courage*. *All Dogs Go to Heaven*, but not *Oliver & Company*. Corruption, but not the void. Errors in judgment, but not honest mistakes. The shape of a bell, but not the shape of a heart. A glimmer, but not a glint. Cookie cutters, but not brownie pans. A scintilla of hope, but not despair. Running, but not walking. Halie Theoharides's *Into the Leaf Gloom*, but not Ben Mirov's *A Few Ideas from My Blackbox*. Manna, but not bread. Gluttony, but not sloth. Songs of Innocence, but not Songs of Experience. The middle, but not the end. Hemming, but not hawing. A good feeling, but not a bad idea. Tissue paper, but not the gift bag it came in. A tattoo, but not a story. Beer, but not wine. Addiction, but not alcoholism. Repression, but not love. Clinical depression, but not clinical anxiety. Green eggs, but not ham. Nikki Grace, but not Laura Dern. Nikki Wallschlaeger, but not Natalie Shapero. *Mulholland Drive*, but not *Inland Empire*. A channel, but not the sea. Bugaboo Creek, but not The Ground Round. Braintree, but not Plymouth. My immediate family, but not my extended family. A wedding reception, but not its venue. A happening, but not an event. Stravinsky's *Le rossignol*, but not Stravinsky's *Le sacre du printemps*. Yellow gold, but not rose gold. Fool's gold, but not the real thing. A professor, but not a teacher. Disappointment, but not pride. A lily-of-the-valley, but not a regular lily. Plainness, but not ostentation. Renaissance, but not Baroque. Camille Rankine, but not Claudia Rankine. Mei-Mei Berssenbrugge, but not (why not??) Wanda Coleman. Countee Cullen, but not Langston Hughes. lucille clifton, but not Hoa Nguyen. Will Alexander, but not W. H. Auden. A villanelle, but not a sestina. Ted Berrigan, but not the poem itself. John Berryman, but not the wind. Sappho, but not the lyre. Inanna, but not Ariana Reines. Eternal recurrence, but not the neutrality of being. Gilles Deleuze, but not Spinoza. Félix Guattari, but not Jacques Lacan. Sibylle Baier, but not Jackson C. Frank. Kennings, but not epithets. The Green Knight, but not Sir Gawain. *Goosebumps*, but not *Animorphs*. K. A. Applegate, but not R. L. Stine. François Villon, but not the rest of traditional French verse. The moon, but not the spirit of the thief. The city streets, but not the city lights. Lawrence Ferlinghetti, but not poetry. A big umbrella, but not the precipitation it protects you from. Withheld reasons, but not invented names. Coffee, but not tea. A hidden landscape, but not the early work of John Ashbery. *Some Trees*, but not *Turandot and Other Poems*. Noelle Kocot, but not Damon Tomblin. Forgotten, but not gone. Settings, but not preferences. Choose-your-own-adventure, but not science fiction. Omeed, but not Daniel or the others. James Turrell, but not the light. Blood, but not anything real. High school, but not kindergarten. Scott, but not Kyle. A little lingering doubt, but not meat consumption. The will to live, but not cute plants. The beginning, but not a warm shadow of wherever we are now. Goodbye, but not forever.

Axe of Despair

assetlessly I fall
afraid of summer,
its moonbeams
oddly hot. There
is a tomorrow here
someplace, full
of vellum & late
apologies like all
your best secrets
—the way the *re*
in *reveal* walks
the knife's edge
of again & *re*
-*versal*, to veil
Once More,
to take the veil
off, I caught
my love for you
in a butterfly
jar, no holes,
the air still
finding its way
out slowly
slowly

Behind their house, behind the back porch
Are the little woods.

—George Oppen

two

Apples, Jug, Iridescent Glass

Its jaw broken, fall
rehearses a troubled speech
of leaves
under cold rain. Ice

is, as yet, a promise
—one you wouldn't hold
anyone to.

Hoosegow

Some people find alcoholism easier
to hide in winter, mistletoe cheeks
magician's-tablecloth roads *that warmth*

—the fever breaks and it's spring. Gardens
begin to crawl back into being
the greenest shared headache of love

after money. In my pocket I carry
a single dandelion
for my enemies. When I visit

and their plot is completely overgrown I
put an arm around them, my face on
fire, and say *hey,* something *still grew here*

Rare Birds of Massachusetts

The farmer's daughter's lover's son
lives in Wellfleet, where the northern flickers
bless Route 6 with muffled drums

each spring. Marconi had a wireless
station there, aimed all the way
across the Atlantic

like a pilgrim in reverse,
backing up over history, bad plumbing
or the car over the corpse

of Pasolini in that Coil song
or real life—the cartoon-red tomato
on the Pastene can

fresh off a truck from where else,
Canton, or the New
England Coffee factory

in Malden that gives every sunrise
notes of smoke
and extremely burnt caramel. The son

was one
of the most beautiful people
I had ever seen, he made me speak

badly and break my lines
in obvious ways, on nouns
and verbs, I hated

feeling so simple
because what is more humiliating
than to be reminded

the thing you want
most in life has only one
part, one speaking role? John

Wieners's god is like this,
his sound always getting stolen
or taken away, like the state

would take your child
if you nailed him to a tree. I
desperately wanted not to be

nervous, to know
my lines & deliver them with care
+ thoughtful originality

on cue, bus service replacing
trains from JFK/UMass to Quincy Center
because as with radio

waves sometimes a little help is needed
to get where one is going:
Gloucester, Manchester

-by-the-sea, DDPerks,
a private beach where white seagulls
scream & scream & nothing happens

to them. A bookstore. Tons

& tons of Olson. Ice
cream places with names like Friendly's

& absolutely no love lost between
motorists. Inexplicably many trucks
and above them, one white-faced storm

petrel making
its statistical pilgrimage
over the Cape Islands, enough

lenses open below to keep the enthusiasts
twittering for another year.
Not that I blame them,

waiting to see
is half the magic of being alive
—Frank O'Hara en attente

du *Polish Rider* with Vincent
(i.e. *prevailing, conquer,*
& how many Francis middle names

on the South Shore)
or the big wave you knew
was coming with the storm surge,

wrong coast to surf it
but right one to photograph
& submit it to the glossy

magazines. Sylvia Plath
assiduously sent her work out,
Ted's too, her mom helped

& still the rejections poured in
like seawater. Enough to stare at the tides
until a body washes up

so you can crawl into it & pretend
to live. Holding a shell
you can hear the surface

of the moon, the gray
silence cats know when they're sleeping
& debtors know when the doorbell

rings, metaphorically,
since there are apps for that now.
If you open the door it's the son,

if you leave it unanswered it's the thief
on either side. Tongue in your ear
either way. Like a patient

identified without a label, song
of the toe tag, *Venereology*
being *not*-a-death-metal-record

Masami Akita needed
to listen to a lot of death metal records
to make—death like Ovid,

as change, not death
as an end
at all

Zum weißen Engel

Like ice in the poems of Sir Thomas Wyatt

Or a minimal black metal ring

Glinting at the bottom of a vat of honey

I have forgotten all tactics

The deer that just watches an oncoming car

Attentively

Is my sister

The fly that descends into the apple

Cider vinegar

With one drop of dish soap

Is my love

Possum Heaven

and the gone little soul on the side of the road said,
one day I will be part of a flower

The Collected Poems
of Paul Blackburn

David Bowie
singing "I've
got drama,
can't be
stolen" Claire
-Louise Bennett
writing "I
discovered early
on in
life that
the right
music can
lend a
glamorous edge
to even
the most
dismal circumstances"
Rosie Stockton
writing "but
parallel our
songs, /
parallel &
breathing" Alice
Notley writing
"Apply the
geranium lipstick,
and deviate"
It all
fits, Paul
it all

feels like
the choristers
on risers
heads toward
heaven a
piano on
tired legs
accompanying I
have a
voicemail from
my mom
the oranges
smooshed into
each other
in their
bag I
hope the
finds are
all right
Nick said
he'll tell
me how
to get
his books
I still
have to
PayPal Mike
for the
painting all
creation ticks
over sucking
blood living
in the

tall grasses
lyric memory
troubadour poetry
stained glass
circus wine
rhubarb dry
& not
too sweet

I Tell The Ghost Of Georg Trakl I'm Sad
The Poems Are Not Coming Out Well

I would rather stare
into the abyss than learn
anything. I won't

say this in job
interviews. You broke
a long covenant

when you said I
in the first line, Georg
said. He told me

off without interest,
like he was
being paid to.

Look, the casual moon.

Poems for Mark

But the sad hotels are full
—Mark Kirschen

1

Pain
Did it make you

2

You know

3

Turn on
The radio

4

The sister
Experience
To having
A soul, bats
Fly out
Over the
Small pond

The little
Skips they make
Catching bugs
For food

That's how
Easily
I think
Of you

5

The second it's said
It enters into
A bucket of saying

Green leaves &
Christmas trees

Animal heaven

6

The river

7

8

Do mosquitoes make mistakes

Like in the experiment
Where they cannot stop
Drinking blood

Is that a mistake

9

I don't think
You wrote
About the moon
Even once

Marianne Moore

The knight asks, stellarly, if he can
Cleave gulls into nü shapes
W/which to pepper our cracked sky like

Mastodon on vinyl, or maybe aging
Into a mirror made of teenagers. I flaw
Whilst winsome and make breakfast

My priority, flowing down the river
Of the average workday *completely*
Unafraid; listen for speeches,

They're how you know a character
Is in love. If you notice the actor
Making choices that's because we

Needed that model of how to take
A snowflake on your tongue and
Shepherd it fully to meltdown. It is

Thine, the Renaissance painting of changing
My mind, and it predates the invention
Of chiaroscuro by ~-500 years.

Feelin' Fine

On the day the canned tarantula expires
Arguably for the second time, a meadow
Enters a poem as a transitional image
While short *i*'s, like kindergartners, line up
To go outside. The algorithm is winning
Because it is bringing you what you like,
The Matrix starring a sun-dried tomato,
A bestselling book made of worms, etc.—

there's a fever garden where you can forgive
anyone for anything, and the bodies
piling up in it are feeling fine, the dynamic
rating system they use to give feedback
has been hovering around a 4.2/5 for years:
mostly agreeable, with a few curmudgeons

Pack My Box With Five Dozen Liquor Jugs

The falcon is directed by an arm,
Begins Laura Jensen's poem "Memory"
& then my head wants to go all *And*
I hunched in its belly till my wet fur froze.,
For some reason, but that's Randall
Walking in the mummification
Poem so that Thomas James & Grace
Lake could run, maybe more like a
Stream then, or a river, Anna
You deep deep mystery what are you
Saying in a line like *My little radish, am*
I neglectful enough?, Sufjan too cracking
My heart like a robin's egg
With "my little Versailles", an all-time
Great trick bc Versailles isn't little
At all, *like why don't you get that*
it's only a trick that the moon is small?,
Ariana Reines, I didn't know which side
Of the street the printer's was on
Until I saw the other side
Was the Holy Cross Cemetery
& Mausoleum, we do not have enough
Money to pay for the whole
Print run so now we are tethered
To the future of money
Aka in debt
Aka in something poems alone
Don't solve

Icy Tower

Googling "how many chambers
does the human heart have"

now I understand why it was called
Enter the Wu-Tang (36 Chambers)

9 members times the chamber
unit rate Harold & Andy Capp

both had hats that covered their eyes
little Tiresii of flavor & elevation

I don't know where this is going
except that earlier today I did

try to pin down that knife
's edge feeling I have about sound

how my whole way of being is split
between this unmoored nothing

feeling & the opposite
feeling of wanting to make

just the right noises like singing
in the car there are no stakes

but the need to do it right
to do right by it to get the words

& the key & the feeling correct
it consumes

(in a world with infinity money & time
I thought about how I'd take

voice lessons just to do less
violence to the songs I love)

my hat cocked all weird from hitting
the roof of the car trying to fix

my posture breathe from the di
aphragm do something with the Garden

head/Leave Me Alone transition
that respects Jeff Mangum

's lung capacity Ray & I
used to belt Holland 1945 in the car

on the way back from school
I couldn't really do it on pitch my

head voice stretched
to a fragile shriek

on empty rings around your heart
the world just screams & falls

apart from the terrible bits
I'm really going to miss teaching

I feel like a complete moral failure
for leaving to wrangle computers

but also if I kept doing it maybe
I'd've just faded into nothing

like neutral gases taking over the ox
ygen in your lungs without your body

ever knowing chamber music
feat. organs, or a song in reverse

Isinglass

The grass is tall enough to ride the wind
without an adult. Big problems hide there,
taking their shifts at the invisible factory
where the corn is processed. Today to work
I am wearing a garland of cinnamon flowers.
Something touches my neck and it is like
ornament becoming essence, a Little Tree
air freshener hung on a Douglas fir, but I'm
not proud enough or that tall or I've gained
too much weight that isn't just moral,
I feel ashamed because I can *see* it, the air
sauntering through & with the feather reeds
at the tips of the switchgrass, *don't quit
your day job*, a wad of gum in a satin glove.

Shadow Barbarian (long mix)

Poets should be smart but I've been drinking
Rolling Rocks since *Mare of Easttown*

I think I like the moon because
Whether it is full

As a diaper or new
As a budding love the 0

On a fresh-minted ten it is not being
Changed, really, by the earth

& sun's banter
Not made coin or clean

If I look through the bottom
Of my green bottle (now

The only glass
In the RR production process

Since Anheuser-Busch bought
Them out—they no longer finish

The beer in glass tanks, nor do they make it
Anymore in Old Latrobe)

I can see it, cut
From whole whitish cloth & hung up

To dry on a doorknob in the night sky
Giving a searing, honest performance

As someone who at a postponed reunion
Recognizes light

But does not remember her name
& here she comes with two beers & a smile

Philosophy

I just want you to understand that if you took every jellyfish who
had ever died in the sea, and not just the visible ones washed up
ashore, no, even the ones who lived and perished in total obscurity,
if you took all their gelatinous inertia rocked by the waves it's
maybe the beginning of an approximation of how my heart has
felt for fourteen years of looking at you. And of course that's like
the most American thing I could possibly do, wrap mass death up
in the matter of an individual heart, but like one tree alone at the
height of a hill offering high noon's only shade for a quarter mile
around I'm stuck with it, I'm carving secrets in the bark because
I'm a dog for you, I'm backwards, yesterday I forgot my own name

Confusion Matrix

I went to the water
reclamation facility
to ask if they had any
jobs. It was a thunderous
need, to feel like I touched
something that helped
people live. They taught me
the sequence, raw
to effluent, effluent to
reclaimed, I paid into the state
retirement system, my children
saw the rain that recharged
the groundwater, and when I died
there was weeping
and inexpensive cake

Where Stars Make Dreams
and Dreams Make Stars

To write poetry you need to eat
to a point where you feel

kind of sick, pumpkin ice cream or
looking at something

you shouldn't for too long—
I don't know, barking

at the moon? Rachmaninoff
in stereo? Come on Tom

you must have a less white
example. The fire we started

with all those Catholic newspapers
—it didn't burn hot or long enough

to keep the birds / from stealing in

Gethsemane

I'm too tired to write a story
about a YouTube Scaled Abuse
Analyst, & maybe you are too
tired to read it, so here
is an outline instead: Tim wakes up
at 3:37AM he's on call
some terrible sequence
of things has been posted
and he, Tim, the Desensitized,
bands together with the algorithms
to try to stop one kid from seeing
whatever heinous thing is in
the video(s). Also it's Mother's Day
and his little independent
contracting entity is called 30Ag
and it's a running gag
whether it's pronounced "thirty agg"
like Virginia Tech or "30 A.G."
like a little mishearing of the year
Jesus starts his ministry.
The story doesn't work because either
a) I have to think up something horrible
to be in the video(s) or
b) I Infinite Jest it and the video
is an unknowable black box, for to know it
is already to be lost, & neither
of those gets me far enough to want
to continue with it, even though I think
it's a good premise, the idea
of the scaled abuse analyst as a real
job gels so cleanly with my own

experiences on websites full of terrible
things when I was younger,
the casual infliction
of evil through depersonalized means
that now is just part of the fabric
of internet existence, you
can hardly avoid it, this guy on Twitter
with two ⊞s in his display name
liked a poem I posted and I saw
his pinned tweet was a blog post: "How
To Protect Your Family
From Adult Content" I'm thinking a Playskool
bucket meeting the mid-Atlantic
when you read Houellebecq
his poems have this kind of stuff
happening on trains, sidewalks
the seeing of something
a certain type of mother would deem
unclean
annunciation's opposite
Houellebecq's poems are oddly tender
for every "Nous avons passé
la nuit sans délivrance" there is also
"J'ai toujours eu l'impression
que nous étions proches,
comme deux fruits
issus de la même branche."
Surprisingly green flowers of early May
coffee late
in the morning, the fog already burned
off the mountain
I used to think A.D. meant After
Death but then with the B.

C. meaning Before Christ what
years did he live?
That actually wasn't enough
of a problem to change
my mind about how it worked
it made total sense that someone could live
outside numbered years that a religion would
accept
its earthly King by not counting time
until after, like a flood
of gossip after the party, like communism
after the party, like cleaning up
rivers and other bodies
of fresh water away
my iniquity
like a Razor
scooter to the shin
drawing blood
& a little bone & a few views
before being taken down
a few pegs
to pray

Headaches at Night

best free online tax software
septic tank flushing
burritos near me
"Laura Gilpin" "Universe"
pain in back of head persistent
jobs you can do after teaching
easiest programming languages to learn
how to say SQL
drywall repair near me
filetype:pdf "Laura Gilpin" "calf"
what day is Mother's Day

Xenakis

Hovering, a jump
rope snaked through
stars, pattern mid-
skip changing like a
fortune, five four
three two one and
a kiss at the end.

Originated

Sometimes you think of these little stories
(would make sense of why you were down
there so long, getting a roll of paper
towels, one hand in the internet & one hand
accessory to nervous autophagy you'll feel
in the quick tomorrow while you're trying
to scrape some last burnt bit off the bottom
of a rounded pan, can't corner it, scratching
up the sink, & just this small shard
of old food slips under & in like an injection
on *2* instead of *3*, which if you remembered
your hangman's paradox you should've
expected, *he's coming on Tuesday* you said,
with the conviction of not really thinking
long enough to understand) & quickly
you forget, under porch light the apple's fist
of water cut into pieces for the possums

Acknowledgments

Thanks to the editors of the following publications, where some of these poems first appeared:

"Saddest Factory" at *ONE ART: a journal of poetry*

"I Don't Know, Black Fog?," "[sorry I'm here now]," "Poems for Mark," "Confusion Matrix," & "Headaches at Night" at the Neutral Spaces blog

"Reflection" at *Salt Water Zine*

"*Pierrot lunaire*" at *E·ratio*

"coign of vantage" in *Complete Sentences* from Broken Sleep Books

"The Virginia Opossum" & "Rare Birds of Massachusetts" in *Some States* for the 2023 Ghost City Press Summer Micro-Chapbook Series

"[Feeling adulthood's sequence of tasks]" & "[I proved I didn't have the stomach for being]" at *Vanity*

"Song of Restoration" & "What Can & Cannot Pass Thru The Green Glass Door" at *Hobart*

"Hoosegow" at *Back Patio Press Zine*

"Marianne Moore" at *Moist Poetry Journal*

"Feelin' Fine" in *Mid/South Sonnets* from Belle Point Press

"Icy Tower" at The Poetry Hotline

"Isinglass" at *HAD*

"Gethsemane" at *unstamatic*

"Xenakis" at *Blazing Stadium*

Listen:

About the Author

Tom Snarsky is the author of the chapbooks *Threshold* (Another New Calligraphy) & *Complete Sentences* (Broken Sleep), as well as the full-length collection *Light-Up Swan* (Ornithopter Press). He lives with his wife Kristi and their cats in the mountains of northwestern Virginia.

www.ingramcontent.com/pod-product-compliance
Lightning Source LLC
Chambersburg PA
CBHW022157080426
42734CB00006B/478

9 781942 723141